First Facts®

LEARN ABOUT ANIMAL BEHAVIOR

ANIMALS
THAT
LIVE IN
GROUPS

BY KELSI TURNER TJERNAGEL

Consultant:
Bernd Heinrich, PhD
Department of Biology
University of Vermont, Burlington

CAPSTONE PRESS
a capstone imprint

First Facts is published by Capstone Press,
1710 Roe Crest Drive, North Mankato, Minnesota 56003.
www.capstonepub.com

Library of Congress Cataloging-in-Publication Data
Tjernagel, Kelsi Turner.
  Animals that live in groups / by Kelsi Turner Tjernagel.
    p. cm.—(First facts. Learn about animal behavior)
  Includes bibliographical references and index.
  Summary: "Discusses animals that live in groups and their behaviors"—Provided by publisher.
ISBN 978-1-4296-8413-2 (library binding)
ISBN 978-1-4296-9308-0 (paperback)
ISBN 978-1-62065-257-2 (ebook PDF)
  1. Animal societies—Juvenile literature. I. Title.

  QL775.T56 2013
  591.7'82—dc23   2012002131

Editorial Credits
Christine Peterson, editor; Alison Thiele, designer; Svetlana Zhurkin, media researcher;
    Laura Manthe, production specialist

Photo Credits
Alamy: Bill Bachman, 13, Images of Africa Photobank, 5, Photoshot Holdings, 10, Robert Harding
Picture Library, 18, Steve Bloom Images, 14; Dreamstime: Peter Betts, cover, Sven Arndt, 9;
iStockphoto: Peter Malsbury, cover (inset), back cover, 1; Newscom: World Pictures/Rick Strange,
17; Shutterstock: Eliks (background), throughout, Skynavin, 6, Steffen Foerster Photography, 21,
therocketbaby (zebra pattern), throughout

Essential content terms are **bold** and are defined at the bottom of the spread where
they first appear.

Printed in the United States of America in North Mankato, Minnesota.
042012   006682CGF12

TABLE OF
CONTENTS

Strong Bonds

An elephant quietly munches grass on the **savanna**. It soon spies a lion hiding in the brush. The elephant sounds a warning. Quickly, the elephant herd forms a circle to protect each other. Like elephants, many other animals live in groups. Animals in groups help each other find food and care for each other. Some animal groups keep each other safe from **predators**.

savanna: a flat, grassy area of land with few or no trees
predator: an animal that hunts other animals for food

Forming Groups

Animal groups form in many ways. Some come together to find a new home. When a honeybee hive is too crowded, the group **swarms**. Half the worker bees leave the hive. They search for a new home.

Animal Fact!

Groups of bees beat their wings to cool the hive on hot days.

swarm: leaving a hive to form a new group

7

Family Matters

Some animals live together their entire lives. Elephants live in family groups with up to 30 animals. Sisters, mothers, grandmothers, and even great-grandmothers live together for life. The oldest female elephant is the **matriarch**. She leads the herd. Elephants help each other find food. They care for sick members and protect the young.

matriarch: the female leader of an elephant herd

Animal Fact!

Male elephants live with the herd until they are about 13 years old. Then they leave to live alone.

Animal Fact!

Herring live in schools all their lives. Light reflects from their silvery scales making them blend together. Predators can't pick one fish out of the school.

Time to School

Other animals gather in groups for short periods of time. About 4,000 kinds of fish swim together in schools. Schools range in size from a few fish to millions of fish. Most fish gather in schools for only part of their lives. Fish often form groups when **spawning**.

spawn: to lay eggs in large numbers

Caring for
Each Other

Animals living in groups take care of each other. **Budgerigars** live together in flocks of thousands of birds. They huddle close to each other for warmth. They **preen** each other's feathers. They roost together to spot danger.

budgerigar: a small, brightly colored Australian parrot

preen: to clean and arrange feathers with a beak

Animal Fact!

Emperor penguins huddle together for warmth in cold weather. So much heat can be trapped in the group that steam may rise.

Learning Together

Some animal groups train their young for survival. Young chimpanzees are great copycats. They watch adults and copy their behaviors. Mother chimpanzees are the main teachers for their young. By watching their mothers, young chimpanzees learn to catch termites. They learn to swing through trees and build nests.

Animal Fact!

A grown wolf pup leaves its birth pack to start a new pack.

Safety in Numbers

Animal groups guard members from predators. Gazelle herds graze together. They all keep watch for predators. If danger is near, a gazelle leaps high in the air. Its legs are pointed down. The leap warns the herd. Others in the herd see the high-flying signal. They quickly run away.

Animal Fact!

A gazelle can run up to 40 miles (64 kilometers) per hour to escape predators.

Food for All

Animals in a group help each other hunt and gather food. Meerkats live in **colonies** of up to 40 animals. They hunt for scorpions, grubs, and beetles during the day. Guards sit at the highest point searching for enemies. At the first sign of danger, the guards bark out a warning. The entire group zips down into their burrows.

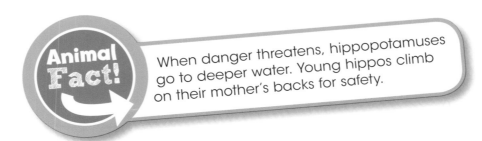

Animal Fact! When danger threatens, hippopotamuses go to deeper water. Young hippos climb on their mother's backs for safety.

colony: a group of the same kind of animal

Learning about Animal Groups

Scientists study animals in groups to learn more about their behavior. Scientists use different tools to gather clues. They use radio transmitters to track groups of moving penguins. Scientists learn about chimpanzees by watching and recording how they act. These methods help scientists understand animal behavior.

Animal Fact!

Dolphins will push a sick or hurt dolphin to the water's surface. The sick dolphin can then breathe.

Amazing but True!

Flamingos love company. A million or more flamingos live in the Great Rift Valley of Africa. Currently, this gathering is the largest known bird flock. The birds gather at the valley's lakes for food and to mate.

Glossary

budgerigar (BUHJ-uh-ree-gahr)—a small, brightly colored Australian parrot

colony (KAH-luh-nee)—a group of the same kind of animal

matriarch (MEY-tree-ahrk)—the female leader of an elephant herd

predator (PRED-uh-tur)—an animal that hunts other animals for food

preen (PREEN)—to clean and arrange feathers with a beak

savanna (suh-VAN-uh)—a flat, grassy area of land with few or no trees

spawn (SPON)—to lay eggs in large numbers

swarm (SWORM)—to leave a hive to form a new group

Read More

Harasymiw, Therese. *Meerkats*. Animals That Live in the Grasslands. New York: Gareth Stevens Pub., 2011.

Kalman, Bobbie. *An Animal Community*. My World. New York: Crabtree Pub. Co., 2010.

Mack, Lorrie. *Animal Families*. New York, DK Pub. 2008.

Internet Sites

FactHound offers a safe, fun way to find Internet sites related to this book. All of the sites on FactHound have been researched by our staff.

Here's all you do:

Visit *www.facthound.com*

Type in this code: 9781429684132

Super-cool stuff!
Check out projects, games and lots more at
www.capstonekids.com

Index